ADVAN

M000038958

These poems of Julie Babcock pulse staccato with keen, austere observation. They blurt out, find reason and dream. Childhood and adolescence are here, always true and unnerving. Ohio, the state of—as character and point of view, dividing and multiplying—makes a funny/sad, most formidable thread. This is a poet of the real and the surreal. Or rather, she's discovered a rich terrain between these two points of wonder. Babcock writes of wishing to find "a gadget" in a store "that changes time." But her poems already do that for us.
> —Marianne Boruch, author of *Cadaver Speak*

These poems are short and precise, thoughtfully uncluttered, but they contain myths and fairy-tales. There is something of those terrifying Grimm Brothers in here, and those troubled classical gods, yet there's also room enough for a heart-breaking Disney. There is an Ohio that is everywhere, yet is, still and forever, Ohio. There is laughter, fear, hope and a vision that is read in "carefully folded notes from the stars." Julie Babcock's vision is wild and smart, utterly unique.
> —Keith Taylor, author of *If the World Becomes so Bright*

Press the play button these poems say, like an old cassette, as we wind and wend and rewind passed the "remainders of barns" though the back roads and small towns and playgrounds of Julie Babcock's ode to her home state blaring Chrissie Hynde and Billy Idol. But these poems are far from simply narrative, more darkly lyrically brief and almost Eastern European in their approach. Mixing pop culture, history, fairytale, and anthropomorphic metaphorical constructions , suck as "Ohio tightens her bow and strings," Babcock shows a range rarely seen in one American collection of poetry. This beautiful and moving book with its praise poems and most importantly elegies to that which has passed and passing, plants us firmly in the hallowed and halo'd hole of Ohio's human heart, asking us "Where are you going now?/The trees around us/full of squirrels larger than cats/the diagonal pathways/leading in all directions.

—Sean Thomas Dougherty, author of *All I Ask for is Longing: New and Selected Poems*

Autoplay is a dizzying compendium, a secret textbook that doesn't leave much out, all of it converging to form a clear whole picture. The poems burst with traces of both personal and national geography, of public and private history. A playground, a kiss, the topography of Ohio. Julie Babcock writes with a compass and a diary close at hand, expertly guiding us to emotional ground again and again.

—Nate Pritts, author of *Right Now More Than Ever*

In *Autoplay*, Julie Babcock notes that bird songs "are full of declaration"—and her poems feel much the same. However, she cloaks her precise observations of everyday life in dynamic metaphors, giving us both "diamonds and cold triangles" throughout this masterful collection. Mapping a personal Midwest, particularly Ohio, Babcock traverses both inner and outer landscapes, boldly discussing the failed myth of return to a never really innocent childhood, as well as the fluidity of adult pain. Her chiseled and gem-like language create poems like the stacks of mirrored tile one speaker receives: they cut and they shine. Either way, they are unlikely to be forgotten.

—Christine Butterworth-McDermott, author of *Woods & Water, Wolves & Women*

Welcome to Ohio, populated by horses and astronauts, wolf moons and changelings. In *Autoplay*, the American Midwest buzzes with mystery, and our guide is a poet of deft lyricism and graceful wit. So let yourself go, dear reader, because, as Julie Babcock writes, "To dream is to let go," and these poems—full of heartache, wonder and awe—dream spectacularly.

—Matthew Olzmann, author of *Mezzanines*

Julie Babcock's first poetry collection is a wonder. Bringing together everything from Billy Idol to Philomel, these poems' brilliant turns twist with a darkness and haunting hilarity rarely seen in a poet so young. *Autoplay* makes the state of Ohio not just a place of historical concern, but a character in its own right, witness to the joys and terrors of aliveness. At the same time, Babcock uses myth and fable to confront cultural assumptions of gender in poems that reinvigorate violated space (the body, the land, the sky) with trauma-forged resilience. "We are all twenty-five feet in the air," Babcock writes. "Anything could happen. Any of us could break or go to fun." The beautiful terror shifting subtly through *Autoplay* will not let you go.

—Alex Lemon, author of *The Wish Book and Happy: A Memoir*

Julie Babcock manages to elevate everyday experiences and to make them into art, not just for those who are already in love with the Midwestern landscape, but for anyone who wishes to ponder the importance of lived moments. At times unsettling, and yet always satisfying, the poems of *Autoplay* draw upon a wide range of references, from Billy Idol to Hamlet, astonishing the reader at every turn.

—Mary Biddinger, author of *A Sunny Place with Adequate Water*

AUTOPLAY

POEMS

MG Press
http://midwestgothic.com/mgpress

Portions of this book originally appeared in *826 Michigan*: "The Changeling"; *The Apple Valley Review*: "Church Crossing"; *The Bakery*: "Johnny Appleseed Proposes"; *The Comstock Review*: "Philomel"; *decomP*: "Big Boy Ohio"; Confrontation: "First Sex"; *The Gingerbread House*: "The Grey Goose," "The Fortuneteller"; *Hayden's Ferry Review*: "Wolfwoman," "Dick and Jane Burn the House Down"; *h_ngm_n*: "Shuffle, Hop, Step"; *The Iowa Review*: "Alice's History Lesson," "Pinocchio"; *No Tell Motel*: "Another Pregnant Chad"; *slipstream*: "Sleeping Beauty," "The Ice Cream Cemetery"; *Sou'wester*: "Astronaut Ohio"; *Spoon River Poetry Review*: "American Flyers," "Multiplication"

ISBN: 978-0988201347

Cover design © 2014 Jeff Pfaller

Cover photo © Sera Hayes

"*I was already dozing off in the shade, dreaming that the rustling trees were my many selves explaining themselves all at the same time so that I could not make out a single word. My life was a beautiful mystery on the verge of understanding, always on the verge! Think of it!*"

—Charles Simic

When Ohio Was the West

For almost two months in 1803
Ohio was the most Western
state in the whole United.
This explains my love of horses.
From my apartment window
I looked for a velvet-muzzled horse
with a brushable mane
to tame and ride bareback
from Shirley Avenue to Coshoctan
to the Storage Facility
where my Filipina friend lived.
She made Easy Bake cake
and thanked us for deliverance
from martial law
weapons and hiding.

She said we were blessed.
My horse and I
with all this freedom.

We listened carefully.
1970's storage shed doors
were aluminum and we bucked
every time they went down.

This sound, the gunshot.

Alice's History Lesson

"Are you listening?"
her sister asks in the middle of
America's colonization, the book
stretched over her prim lap.
They are seated by the Thames
but Alice is supposed to be studying
Boston, where, she believes,
orange marmalade can't possibly be as good.
She watches the daffodils waggle their heads
and waits for her cat to pounce.

That morning Alice plucked
forget-me-nots for Mother
and wrapped them in Father's newspaper.
The wet ink blurred into
ants and delightful miniature paw prints.

"Where's my paper?" her father bellowed
as Alice handed Mother the blooms
and the fat cat rubbed and mewed.

"We don't need to tell," Mother winked
as she peeled front pages from stems
and whirred them down the garbage disposal.
"It's already happened."

Fun Slide

My playground
breaks and changes
from four square courts
to monkey bars
from parking garages
to office doors.

There are bells
and the bathrooms
are missing paper towels.

There are bells
and I teach college on the lawn.
My students form a circle
and ask where I've been
themselves full of meaning
football games and balcony parties
their bags full of laptops
and monster drinks. I say
Where have you been?
and they say *fun*.

I drink from my water bottle–
cold and clear thinking
that moves through my body.
From this riverbank someone
throws in pieces of my life

watches them dissolve or sink
skip or foam.

I was riding to El Dorado
Where?
to Xanadu, to Oz.
I was trout fishing.
What?
I was poling a raft
towards Avalon.

They ask me how old I am.
Whether I know the rapper Mike Miller
whether I am going to see him
whether I drink coffee and have a car.

I ask *Where are you going now?*
The trees around us
full of squirrels larger than cats
the diagonal pathways
leading in all directions.

They are going to Mo-Jo,
to CC Little, to Markley,
Bursley, and Bates. They are
iPodding towards the North Quad.

I am still going
up the rickety ladder
of my fun slide
the one torn down
because it was too high.
Climbing the iron stairs
pebbles in my knees

hair in every direction.

Maybe this time
the scared girl in front
will hold tight to the bar
or maybe she will sail.
The girl behind is so close
I can't step down.

Maybe I say *Get out of my way*
or I hold tight and hang.

We are all twenty-five feet in the air.
Anything could happen. Any of us,
could break or go to fun.

Music Lesson Ohio

Ohio tightens her bow and strings.
She slips her chin against the violin
and wraps her fingers around the neck.
Between the bridge and fret,
there's only an inch of space.
Clear notes jump into
scratches that don't penetrate.
Her teacher says it is hardest
to play softly. *Pianissimo, Ohio.*
Keep off open strings.

Soon she will have a first concert.
She will borrow a white, frothy gown
and sit so straight the back
of the aluminum folding chair
never touches the bow around her waist,
so tall the snap on her new bra stretches.

I will be melody, she vows.
Ohio practices every day.

Shuffle, Hop, Step

Like tripping
into a jump and then
steadying again.
tap, tap. Break. Tap.
That basic YMCA step
I practiced as a girl
sticky from quarter machine candy.

I still do it
because I don't want to fall
and break and x-ray
in that heavy bib of lead
for rectangles of light and transparencies.

My feet keep moving.
Cincinnati with beer and boys
Chicago book blind
Shipwrecked in Michigan.
tap, tap. Break. Tappin'.

I keep watching Debbie Reynolds
in baby blue heels
trying to hang with Gene Kelly.
"Good morning, good morning"
she sings as she jumps on and off tables
up and down flights of stairs,
somersaults off one couch

onto another. Never trained to dance,
she just shows up with grit.
I keep watching her stick the landings
those bloody feet
clicking good morning and catching.

Driving at Midnight

I want to let go when I arrive.
For an open door full of light.
For a lover with a blanket.

This motor thrums and music
points its gauges. Half moons
shine beyond my fingers.

To dream is to let go
and see that all of it
stays in this same lane

and never crashes.
Whatever passes
and doesn't pass flashes into

mirrors and eyes
then shrouds itself
and whispers exits in the dark.

Tecumseh!

Since the premier performance of "Tecumseh!" in 1973, over 2.4 million visitors have witnessed this great out-door play, making it the most popular of its kind in the state of Ohio and entire Mid-Western United States.

—official Tecumseh! website

Ohio loves to be sorry.
She sits in the beautiful spectacle
with galloping horses and American cannons.
The shame of gunfire against arrows.
Tecumseh, she whispers, *keep trying*.

He dies and resurrects for the meet and greet.
Thank you she says as he autographs her playbill.

The Ice Cream Cemetery

It is old as good cemeteries always are
with big trees and vaults and grass
breaking footpaths. Some say ghosts
steal your breath.

After school, children walk
through the cemetery to the dairy
for Rainbow Sherbet and Heavenly Hash.
They recall a little of what teachers say,
that the dead here are famous.
They pass tombs liking this idea,
this famous world underfoot.

They buy ice cream and go back
eating their treats quickly
before they change shape.

Rats

"Trust me,"
Mother whispers to her daughter

as she positions the plastic comb teeth.
A tug, an ouch.

Her daughter.
There are more.

Mother throws a mangled tail on the floor,
goes back to the soft, pink flesh.

A twitch, a claw.
Another squealing nest.

Jonah's Trick

We saw him sucked
into rows of triangular fish teeth
and magically reappear.
Then we wanted it again.

A duck returns from a wolf
by waddling out his panting mouth.
A girl returns from a wolf
by axing through his hairy belly.

It can't always work
which explains the long line of wolves
backstage ducks preening in the wings
extra girls swinging in the rafters.

He is getting too old to stage the sea
wrapped in all that seaweed and salt.
We wait with bottled big fish
for the next spout and breach.

First Sex

When I was thirteen
I stole the Billy Idol cassette
Rebel Yell
and didn't get caught.
It was protected
in a long, plastic case
to stop shoplifters
but my purse was longer
and I escaped to a nearby field
where I sawed with Mom's
cheap steak knife
and set Billy free. Sun
struck his face. No one
knew where I was. No one
in my lifelong, small town.

That night Billy snarled his songs
down my neck.
He was heat and hard spikes
gelled lines of hair, dog leash collar,
especially that upper lip
thrusting and thrusting
as if a drill bit in his mouth
could bust apart everything.

Preparedness

I am in two places at once—
less as a space time traveler
and more as a slow pedestrian
in some metropark cross walk.

I keep repacking my bag
to only include necessities.
Umbrella or water bottle?
Boots or flip flops?
Sweater or striped tankini?

The birds are busy choosing
trees. Their songs are full
of declaration and lust.
They waggle feathers
and puff for each other.

I should have brought a kayak
instead of strapping
this electric generator to my back.
What happens when I'm alone
is a loud swarm of governmental bees.

The Moundbuilders Country Club

The golf course at Moundbuilders is unlike any other in the world. It is designed around famous Prehistoric Native American Earthworks that come into play on eleven of the holes.
—official website of The Moundbuilders Country Club,
located in Newark, Ohio

She points toward the green hills
on the golf course. Two-hundred-year-old
earthworks Hopewell Indians engineered
to calculate the cycle of the moon.
Eight mounds, eight sides of an octagon.

I follow the line of her arm
an arrow raised towards the country
club fence full of diamonds and cold triangles.

Only members see the whole thing
past this six-foot-high hill
sliced with white pavement.

A golf cart goes over. Then
a caddy. I was inside once
I tell her. For a field trip.
Someone's parents belonged.

We lean in until our tanned arms touch.
The fence directs our hands. The fence
tunnels under our feet.

Being Right

doesn't change much.

I wish you could place an ear to a shell
inside an ocean that never spills
and hear me.

Or hear a question mark
a soft beginning that rises
until you decide I could help.

All I have today is a bell
with a heavy clapper.

Amen to Artillery

She sets the encyclopedia on her head.
It is difficult to balance. It slides
off the brink into her hands.

It is annoying to adjust and only think
"heel to toe" as she walks
only softly because she's becoming a lady
not born knowing how to walk across rooms.

A lighter book would be better. Especially
after the double fumble off the brink
through the hands, toward the floor. Heavy
words like a cannonball.

Capture and Release

This small confused mouse.
She only wants to trick him
into this box and move it beyond
the garage and the grate
birds pulled apart to nest.
She only wants to set him free.

He bumps the same corner and she tells him
I locked the cats upstairs.
I am not a cat.

He clonks the wall and squeaks
like a toy with a rubbery tail.

The last time her cat caught a mouse
he mouthed it for a moment then
released it still alive. It was alive
when she boxed and moved him
to the hill by the tree the small body
so still at the moment of liberty.

American Flyers

It's free flag day.
Break off the toothpick end
and a flag is
a blanket, the flag end
a miniature walking stick
or jousting lance.
Stars and stripes
fly and roll
into tiny telescopes,
wave and fold
into horses. Randy
gets a star which makes him
Sheriff, which makes him
Ninja, which makes him a winner
and something to wish on.
The children in the apartment courtyard
have parameters and boundaries.
A blue scrap is moat or sky.
All the bloody lines lead somewhere—
all the white space remains.

The Grey Goose

I.
I was floating alone when they first tried to kill me.
Water lapping against reeds thick with river
mud and fish. I have so many feathers,
I thought, before the gun shot flew.

II.
Then plucked like a daisy.
My white petals
loves me loves me not.
The quills from my body
full with ink that flowed
like water from home. There,
I wrote, I am.

III.
When my ink dried they put me back
into water, closed the lid
and stopped the air.
What remained I counted
numbers that rose and swam together
so beautifully I thought
I might have become a swan.

IV.
The dinner party guests raised their knives
but my skin was too thick
Their sharpened steel couldn't sink.

They brayed and dropped their weapons,
threw their nice chairs and stained everything with wine.

V.
Rumbalide! So many beautiful things
in the garbage! I could have stayed
for centuries in layers of abandoned love.
I lined my splinters with blindfolds. I grew
more quills and ink. Daisies rooted
in water reeds and lids opened
to sunfish. Abandoned love kept whispering
hope so lovely I remembered. Through layers
I cut a tunnel out.

VI.
Back where I belong. Lapping
water against me. Who found another.
How I called to him through white water lilies
where the turtles waited to dry. Where layers
of lake grew tadpoles and filtered sun.
Here I am, Here I am! I called. Because
there is nothing like the shot
of a heart into a heart. Beating wings
against water. Head
going under. Feet sunk in mud.
We tried to stay there forever
where death was a strong song unable to die.
Then these, my children,
hatched to this water all fluffy and free.
Look at them learning to follow!

Bedroom

Hot as a dragon's tongue.
Summer girls think of boys
and caves. How to enter
until limestone drips.

They breathe against the mirror,
draw initials in the vapor,
press their lips to the glass
and laugh at how it feels

like teeth they imagine. Slick
white light before the opening.

The Delivery

is stacks of mirrored glass tile
she never ordered. A gift
with a secret message
from her neighbor or ex.
Childhood friend or foe.

It takes the day
to move them inside.
Some break.
Some cut.

A bead from blood.
Glass from a sand grain.

Autoplay

I am the baby-sitter. She
is snuggled so close
we might be one.
We hear a noise
and flee the house.
"We're safe," I say, as we jump
on the outdoor trampoline.
Double somersaults
of fear, my promise,
"no one else is here."

Then window glass shatters
and we remember I am wrong.
I hold her tight. My ear
heats with her breath. Sometimes
we jump back to the house.
But it never matters. The man
is both inside and outside.

Ohio Apologia

I want to love you to love myself.
The birth stem is a vain cut.
A twin can never divide her wealth.

You said that no blow dealt
could force you in the gutter rut.
I want to love you to love myself.

You said (you said) just how you felt,
played a song then rolled the keyboard shut.
A twin can never divide her wealth.

I planned to go where I'd never melt
into a mold of virgin or slut.
I want to love you to love myself.

I crossed the rivers with my bag of stealth
my story line revised and trussed,
but a twin can never divide her wealth.

You brought me gravel pits and knelt
repeating roads repeating dust.
If I don't love you I don't love myself.
My twin will never divide her wealth.

Wolf Moon

This change in the air—
bright to dim and back again
as if the moon were a gold coin
dropped into a slot
and then pulled back out
by an invisible string
knotted around its fat middle.

Just like that
the money used and reused
this chunk of change
full of fear and love.
Lon Chaney
returning to his father's castle
the forest full of gypsies.

Islet

I used to think silence
was emptiness.
I tried to fill it
but it was like pouring
dirt through a sifter
only the biggest things stuck,
awkward hanging there alone.

Once I found a set of bones
that looked like a human hand
except much larger.
That was because
it was a whale fin.
Under the skin whales have
jointed fingers
and opposable thumbs.

How did a whale
get to my gravel pit?
I sift my bones quietly.
Whales talk in such low frequencies
we miss most of what they say.

Philomel

Arms spread to wings—
the severed tongue forced back
inside a beak.
She is smaller, her heart
beating fast against her breast.
Maybe it's better;
she won't tell.

She won't speak
of the body
pressed against the floor
that took the thrusts, why
we have nightingales.

The song she sings
is a different language.
When women become birds
they sit high
in unreachable trees.

The Witnesses

Broken nails against the underworld
the emergence into landscape.

I wander through these parks
and ask the statues.

Did you see anything?
That day I returned?

Some of the statues say nothing.
Some hold their mouths open
and force out stone.

Construction

I used to think this road
went deeper. The weight of cars,
freights, gravity and rain.
How does it hold
above such a meager core?

All that carries us
a bit of gravel and concrete slab
iced with asphalt. Each morning
I check my mirrors and merge.
Beside me, bulldozers tear and replace.

Solving for X

The train leaves the station
southbound at 5 PST
with two stops:
Memory Mound
and Platform Code
both stops sum total
of something.

The question is when
to arrive. Meaning
always ahead
and so always changed.
"I'm in trouble"
yesterday's news
the memory of a code
already solved
or worsened.

What it would be like
to see someone
crane their neck down the track
and wave a red flag
as we approach together!

Iron bathed in steam.
That face in the window.
Expectations and deliverance.

Chrissie Hynde Returns to Ohio

after all these years looking
badass with the same Fender.

She's touring a new album
and opening a restaurant
in our home state.

I used to listen to her for hours.
I used to dance with her words.
She asks, what changed?

Nothing, I say,
stopping myself
from lame explanation.

We're hungry
so chop onions and sizzle in oil.
We're thirsty
so pour my cheap scotch.

She plays sets
so time to make toasts:
To highways, returns, and Ohio
so rhythmic this clunk of glass.

On the Carousel

She wanted to choose a horse
to match her dress
one that went up and down
and neighed under spinning lights.

Pretty red hair wandering
and then the father's smack.

The choice gone
the old gray horse
littlest of them all
and then the going home.

Three-In-One

Mother holds the doll close
to Baby's face: "Red."
She shakes it: "Red Riding Hood."
Baby likes it. She spits bubbles
and kicks her legs.

Mother flips up Red's dress
and inverts her.
"See, now she's Grandmother."
Baby's big eyes get bigger. Oh no,
where did Red Riding Hood go?
Baby cries. Mother checks the clock
and turns the edge of Grandmother's nightcap.

When Father returns, he takes off his shoes
and holds one while he speaks:
"Finally, we're together."
Mother nods and shakes the limp doll
in screaming Baby's face.
Father tosses his shoe towards the wolf
in the grandmother nightgown:
"I'm changing my clothes," he says and disappears.

The Remainder of Barns

The Ohio Bicentennial Commission's barn painting program started as a unique means of getting free, highly visible advertising.
—Federal Highway Administration

They've been painted again.
200 years
underlined with waving ribbons.
Whatever they were
rolled into new white clothes
and fields of thistle flowers.

Empire

All around her lay
wasted apples that fell
before she came to pluck them.

How many still to drop?
Fruit so close to leaving
bending branches.

Her plastic peck bag
fills and stretches
beyond hope.

This country of hers
wherever she moves
a haywagon.

These tickets and tours
and clapboards by the fence
promising variety.

Children bite
into their first fruits
clear juice dribbling.

"Mine," they say.
Shoes already slicked
with apple mash.

Johnny Appleseed Proposes

Take these remains
and plant them. Don't fight

this land is made
for resurrection.

Roll away the stones
and recall our bodies

grow even as we sleep
branching, budding and pushing open.

Crescents of dirt shift under our nails.
Take my hand—

We will wake in blossoms.

The Changeling

Her parents are out bowling
and the babysitter didn't read
a bedtime story. The forlorn child
waits under the covers remembering.

Perhaps someone will come
and save her. A handsome prince
or her real parents, the ones
she didn't know about until now.
They are better than her bowling parents.
They drink orange pop
and rollerskate on rollercoasters
back to their home in the clouds
where giant oyster shells never close.

Or when they do
the blankets are dandelions
and crickets rub their bows
with sleep dust and raise violins.
All for you, those parents sing
as their willow fingers
rub her back. *This basket
of stars. This life
we will never leave.*

Wolfwoman

"Duality," the mad scientist says
"drives us toward conflicting things."

He unstraps himself
from the examining table.

Through the skylight,
the full moon casts a net.

Behind a heavy door,
something thumps.

He counts on his fingers:
"We want savage and civilized,

masculine and feminine,
active and passive."

His thumb goes out for the finale
"Author and character."

I don't say anything.
We stand in the net of light together

this old underground laboratory
filled with dripping water

and locked doors. More keep appearing

thick iron ones with chains and padlocks.

I want to ask how I got here
when my stomach growls. He grows silent

as my nails click across the slate floor.

Pregnant Chad

They call a school assembly.
It is a boy's name but of course
she is a girl. Her belly
full as the moon under her black t-shirt.

We squeak our seats and wonder
about permanence. What if she
goes on and on being pregnant?
Urinating all the time, unable
to fit into nice jeans.
Will she ever get another chance to choose?
Her silly putty skin rises
over the elastic waistband of her pink skirt.

They dim the lights.
She steps back
and the red, velvet curtains close . . .

The MacGuffin

The sun went down and my friends
grabbed a case of beer and opened the car door.

"Let's go," they said
but I was busy with slight adjustments

to my old, automatic seatbelt.
The box machine ran the window length

and sometimes got stuck in the middle
until the door was shut again.

My friends disappeared toward the gravel pit
as I waited for the whirr from my fickle protecting god.

Big Boy Ohio

gets an apron and nametag.

She rolls pennies. The pie case turns
the color of the moon. She fills
coffee cups and sugar boxes.

She fills half-full ketchup bottles
from half-empty so customers believe
they have new natural tomatoes
boiled down and slipped into glass necks.

"Hey, honey," they say before they order burgers
so neatly she might be a virgin
who sleeps under a field of stars
and soothes cows for the dinner table.

Last Night

I wasn't going to wear
those crazy clothes for nothing.
Leopard leotard and tights
sucked to my lumpy body.
Pinned peacock feathers in my hair
fanning above the high wire.
I didn't fall. All that glitter
got me to the little platform
of congratulations. Then
down the long ladder
as the circus air emptied.
By the time I hit bottom
even the ants had packed.

Black Walnuts

Green pods
fall like grenades from the sky
and still remain closed.

Someday I will undo their membranes
dry shells and harvest meat
before the grubs get them.

Some people crush them with cars
smashing and scattering
bucketfuls of slick green circles.
But I will hold each one
slip the knife in and pull
until my fingers
drip tobacco-colored juice.

Who doesn't want to prove there is a core?
Nuts inside the inside
like nesting Russian dolls
in glass displays. Girls so sturdy
after they are taken apart
they pull themselves back together.

Memory

My childhood
house of yellow
corded wood
on a carport.

A brick fireplace.
A long match.

Church Crossing

Moments before the processional bells
a woman leaves church and crosses
the street. She carries what appears
to be a young child. But all I see
is red coat with white
fluffy fringe around the hood.

How does she know the child
is still there? She holds the coat
with both hands but never looks
to see if the body has slipped out.

Altar boys open the doors
as she crosses the snow shoveled parking lot
and cuts through a melting lawn.

Her steps barely make a print.
Soon there will be
no evidence of either of them.

Pinocchio

"I think therefore I am"
—Descartes

He feels like an ass standing in front of this fairy
a jumble of loose dowel rods and crotchety pins.

She is so blue—bluer than blueberries in milk
bluer than frozen lips. The way
she hovers outside that window. How
can she understand anything
about being human? Who is she
to judge a puppet from a boy? He
is sick of her punishments
for skipping school, gluttony
and whaling. Three strikes
after three swings of his wooden bat.

Don't fairies disappear
if children don't believe?
He closes his eyes.
I don't see you, he warns
as his wooden fingers
splay against the plate glass.

This Store

I didn't want to go home
so I walked into this store.
Maybe to buy something
or see stuff
I didn't know existed
something in the kitchen aisle
or clearance section
by the toys. Maybe a gadget
that changes time.
Hardly anyone is here
and it takes twenty minutes
to find the manager
and ask about watch batteries.
She walks the circle
of the jewelry counter
shaking her head until
I drop my keys.
"You lost something," she says.

Replacement

One day the milk in her breasts dried.
She opened the bottle of apple juice
and poured it into a special cup with a spout.

The spout was longer than her nipple and with bigger holes.
Little baby, little big boy she sang as she placed
him in the high chair.

He slapped the tray and opened his mouth,
flashed one milky white tooth
as she handed him the cup.

Sighing and sucking the contents down
as if all had been desert before. The golden apple juice
sweet and lightly flowing through plastic. Her nipples drier
than sand.

The Porcelain Christmas Village

Iron bench by church.
She arrives under night light
webbed in cotton snow.

Sugar Plum

The girls wanted to leave
after the wind-up toys
and death of the Mouse King.
They bounce in their seats
and unbraid licorice twists.

You wait for the woman with a real lover
to extend her leg and spin.
She can start and stop
in any position. Her muscles
lengthen her dreams. Her thighs
refuse a nightdress.

The girls fold their programs into fans
as she arches against her partner.
They drop their ticket stubs
and kick paper snowflakes.

She stretches so far you feel a pulse.

Sleeping Beauty

Comatose, the last fairy said,
not dead. She is beautiful
in her hospital bed
plastic tubing curling
through her hair.

Each time the doctor enters
he unties her green gown
and places his stethoscope
between her breasts.
He opens her eyelids
and forces in light.
Not dead he keeps inscribing
on her golden chart. *Beautiful
and not dead.*

He loves her
and knows he can conquer.
Tubes and conductors.
Shining swords in her eyes.

Singles

This, my jewelry box
for lone earrings.

Pieces that pressed
against once smooth skin
and sparkled.

Nights that slipped
into each other
and rolled like waves.

Odyssean pearl.
Golden leaf.
Pomegranate drop.

This myth of return.

The Ride

Someone left a million pennies
by the mechanical horse but the child
wants to run in the rain.

The mother wants strawberries
and a nap. She lifts the wet child
into a cart and wheels him past
the grocery sign: *Pardon our dust.*
Temporary instructions point shoppers
to aisles of milk and rows of grain.

When they return to the rain,
the child remembers the horse. The mother
runs with him in her arms gently
like a handful of strawberries.
She says they can ride tomorrow. She promises
even if the horse has strayed
there will be more signs and pennies.

Car, Time Machine

That jolting kind of travel—
warps and amps leather
like cushions and straps.

All the years in these gears
lights on and flashing
Gonna make it!
To the sign!
To the next sign!

There's damage
but it's taken me this far
and it might get me back.

The Fortuneteller

She opens my hand.
A silver dollar. She bites the coin
then holds it towards the dingy light.
It is proper US mint.
President Kennedy stares sideways
towards the beaded curtain.

I close my hand and she opens it again.
A flower. She plucks it
and we continue. A porch swing.
She sits on it and we keep going
up into the apple trees
with the baby robins in their low slung nests
Anything you want, she says,
and opens my hand again.

Johnny Appleseed Dies

becoming

romance

or

appliances

mythical.

The groceries

in a

few hours

mush

corn and wheat

molasses

voyages

more useful

than the tomahawk

and scalping-knife.

our modest

hero

planted

in

the State of Ohio.

Bright Light

Everyone leaves
and the spotlight fixes me.

Is this a monologue
or a soliloquy? Puck
or Hamlet? Who
is waiting in the wings
watching my lips
telling jokes to each other?

In the pit
the orchestra plays motley:
vibrato of a weeping woman
bass tremors of a memory.
Sometimes crashing cymbals
startle me enough to stare into the brightness.

No mirror.
Only dots dancing.

We Do Whatever

tell today I've heard
young people singing
In an hour come over and we're
twenty-five non-stop.
my picture and I We do whatever
I can't help this
love. I hope to live in
everything.

Dick and Jane Burn Down the House

Dick wipes his snotty nose as he watches the flames.
"Finito," Jane says, "Poof."

Dick shrugs and keeps his eyes on the house.
Already three shirt buttons have popped. His belt
has vanished and his pants slip from his waist
lick his hips, ready to drop.

"I'm going to Vegas," Jane plans, "to learn how to dance.
I'll hijack the next spaceship and travel to Mars." Jane
is bored with this Midwestern fire. Firemen
in puffy yellow suits shout from ladders. A Dalmatian
chases his tail across the lawn.

"Come on," Jane says, dragging Dick
toward the edge. "Let's show them
how fast we can fly."

Astronaut Ohio

One of the areas in which Ohioans have blazed new trails is spaceflight. According to NASA, 24 astronauts are Ohio natives, with another ten astronauts calling the Buckeye State home at one point in their lives.
—Jon Husted, Ohio Secretary of State, 2010

The future of human spaceflight is bright. You'll hear me say that over and over and over again.
—NASA chief Charlie Bolden at the final shuttle flight launch, 2011

Astronaut Ohio
is leaving. She has packed
her clean underwear and trip tick.
She has said goodbye
to her birthplace and Orville's
before Kitty Hawk, Edison's
before Menlo, Spielberg's
before Close Encounters, Turner's
pre Flying D.

What is left
without Ohio? She is
spelled with arms and sung
in stadiums. Accompanied
by red birds and flags, hill body
rivers and streams. Ohio

in her cheerleader skirt
rolling through the grass
to the white yard line
tangling her apple-scented hair
while her fluffy pompoms fall
to the beat of the rolling rah rah.
Her glossy lips cheering. Vanity
vanity, vanity fair.

She is worship
with a new altar song
white and everlasting.
Pearls in her ears
combs in her hair
diamonds flashing from her fingers. Look!
she comes down the aisle pretending
she's been nowhere.

Carried once
by a stream reflecting the moon.
Before Armstrong and Apollo
before Appleseed. Shimmering light
over what was here but is now there.

She promises to pyramid through the atmosphere
jacknife through galaxies
write carefully folded notes from the stars.

Message in a Bottle

What she wrote was carried by multiple currents.
Wind, water, the cycle of the moon.
What she wrote was already changed
by anyone who might have found it.
Maybe someone with fingers small enough
to slip down the bottle neck
but too young to read the words
who would see the message as a clue
to a larger mystery, who would carry it
in a pocket until it was time to unfold.

Or maybe someone with fingers too big
to reach inside would guess what she wrote
and make her words more tender,
more like a love letter to touch at night
when no one else arrives.

ACKNOWLEDGMENTS

Gratitude and love to fellow writers and friends Danielle LaVaque-Manty, Jennifer Solheim, Megan Levad, and David Ward. A giant shout-out to the Midwestern Gothic team, especially Robert James Russell, Jeff Pfaller, and Christina Olson. Beyond words, Matthew Kelley, always still here.

Grateful acknowledgment is made to the following publications where these poems, in one form or another, first appeared:

826 Michigan: "The Changeling"
The Apple Valley Review: "Church Crossing"
The Bakery: "Johnny Appleseed Proposes"
decomP: Big Boy Ohio
The Comstock Review: "Philomel"
Confrontation: "First Sex"
The Gingerbread House: "The Grey Goose," "The Fortuneteller"
Hayden's Ferry Review: "Wolfwoman," "Dick and Jane Burn the House Down"
h_ngm_n: "Shuffle, Hop, Step"
The Iowa Review: "Alice's History Lesson," "Pinocchio"
No Tell Motel: "Another Pregnant Chad"
slipstream: "Sleeping Beauty," "The Ice Cream Cemetery"
Sou'wester: "Astronaut Ohio"
Spoon River Poetry Review: "American Flyers," "Multiplication"
"Johnny Appleseed Dies" is an erasure of the 1871 *Harper's New Monthly* article by W.D. Haley "Johnny Appleseed—A Pioneer Hero"

"We Do Whatever" is an erasure from Sheila Heti's novel *How Should a Person Be?*

CPSIA information can be obtained at www.ICGtesting.com
Printed in the USA
LVOW07s0245121114

413256LV00003B/235/P

MOCHA

THE PUPPY PLACE

Don't miss any of these other stories by Ellen Miles!

THE PUPPY PLACE

MOCHA

ELLEN MILES

SCHOLASTIC INC.

For Kim and Carolyn, and Mocha, of course!

ISBN 978-0-545-46240-2

Cover art by Tim O'Brien
Original cover design by Steve Scott

12 11 10 9 8 7 6 5 4   13 14 15 16 17/0

Printed in the U.S.A.   40

First printing, December 2012

CHAPTER ONE

"Wow, look at that one." Charles stared as his mom steered the van past another huge house, high on a hill. "It's like a castle! I don't remember any of these giant houses from last year."

"They all sprang up like mushrooms." Mom shook her head. "This area sure has changed."

It was a few days before Thanksgiving, and the Petersons were on their way to visit Uncle Stephen, Aunt Abigail, and Charles's cousins Becky and Stephanie, who lived way out in the country.

Last time they'd come, this road had been a quiet lane with fields of corn, grazing cows, and apple orchards on either side. This time everything looked different. New roads had been carved through what used to be fields and forests, and gigantic houses dotted the open land.

"Meadow Acres." Dad snorted as he read a sign near one cluster of brand-new houses. "Not anymore, it isn't. Stephen told me there had been a lot of development here. Rich people from the city, mostly. They think the area is just charming, perfect for a weekend getaway home."

"You mean people don't even live in those gigantic houses full-time?" asked Lizzie, Charles's older sister. "That's not fair, when some people don't have any homes at all."

Dad nodded. "You're right, it's not fair," he said.

"Not fair, not fair," chanted the Bean, Charles's younger brother, from his car seat. He bounced and waved his fists in the air.

Buddy chimed in with a few happy barks. Charles put his arm around his brown-and-white puppy, who sat cuddled between Charles and Lizzie, strapped into a travel harness. Buddy leaned against Charles and snuffled into his ear. Charles kissed Buddy's nose and sighed happily as he scratched the heart-shaped white patch on Buddy's chest. The world wasn't fair, but at least he had Buddy, the best puppy in the world.

Charles and Lizzie had wanted their own puppy forever, but no matter how much they had begged, their parents had said no. Finally, though, Mom and Dad had agreed that the family could foster puppies, taking care of each one just until they found it the perfect forever home. Soon Charles and Lizzie had proven how responsible they could be. When Buddy came along, the whole family fell in love with him, and Mom and Dad decided that the family was ready for a dog of their own.

Now Charles hugged Buddy closer. "We're almost there," he whispered into the pup's ear. He felt a little twinge in his belly as Mom turned up the road that led to his cousins' big old farmhouse.

Lizzie loved to travel. She was always excited to go anywhere. But Charles liked his own house, his own things, and his own bed. He never felt quite comfortable when he was away from all that. Still, having Buddy with him was like bringing a little bit of home. All Charles had to do was touch Buddy, and he felt better.

"I wonder what Becky is up to these days," Lizzie said. "She's always getting into adventures."

Charles felt the twinge again. He liked Becky a lot. His cousin was funny and smart and good at solving mysteries. Charles liked playing detective with her. Their most successful case had been when they figured out the truth about Flash, a border collie puppy who had mysteriously appeared at Becky's house. But sometimes Becky was a little *too* adventurous.

"Remember when they were visiting last spring and she dared you to climb that big maple tree?" Lizzie asked. "I'll never forget the look on your face when you got up to that high branch and couldn't figure out how to get back down."

"Lizzie, don't tease," Mom said. "Thankfully Charles wasn't hurt, but that whole business wasn't the least bit funny. I was worried sick until he was back on the ground."

Charles sighed and looked out the window. Mom was right. It hadn't been funny. It had been scary, really scary. "Hey, look at *that* place," he said, trying to change the subject. The weak winter sun had nearly set and long shadows crept along the snow-covered ground, but he could just make out a tall iron gate flanked by giant stone pillars. Beyond it, a driveway marked by tall trees on either side wound up the hill and disappeared into a forest of pine trees. "Imagine how gigantic that house must be, if that's just the gate."

"I'll bet your aunt and uncle aren't too thrilled about the way their town is changing," Mom said. "After all, they moved out of the city so they could have a simpler life." She turned the van up a long, bumpy unpaved driveway. "Here we are," she said as they pulled up in front of the old farmhouse. "At least their place hasn't changed at all."

Charles's aunt, uncle, and cousins came out onto the porch when the van pulled up. "Hello! It's so great to see you all," said Aunt Abigail. Amid a lot of hugs and "look how you've grown's," everyone helped unload the van. Soon all their stuff was piled in the front hallway: extra pots and pans for cooking the big holiday dinner, suitcases, Charles's special favorite pillow, Mom's knitting stuff, Lizzie's sleeping bag, the Bean's toy fire truck, Buddy's bed and food dishes, Dad's hiking boots.

"We can only stay a few weeks," Mom joked, looking around at the huge pile.

"You're welcome as long as you want to be here," said Aunt Abigail. "You're my favorite sister-in-law, remember? And I'm so glad you were able to come a few days early. Stephen doesn't believe the weatherman, but if this ice storm they're predicting does show up, nobody will be going anywhere later this week."

Charles shifted from foot to foot as he half-listened to the grown-ups talking. Delicious cooking smells drifted in from the kitchen, and Charles's stomach grumbled. How long would it be until supper? He caught Becky's eye and rubbed his tummy while he made a funny face.

She started to laugh, but her giggles were drowned out by a loud knocking at the door.

Aunt Abigail raised her eyebrows. "Who could that be?" she said as she opened the door. There, in the shadows just beyond the yellow glow of the hall light, stood a tall dark man in a black suit.

"Hello," he said. "I'm hoping you can help me out."

When the man took a step forward into the light, Charles gasped.

The stranger on the doorstep had a puppy in his arms.

CHAPTER TWO

For a moment, nobody said a word. They all stood gaping at the stranger on the doorstep. Charles noticed his shiny black hair, his silky red tie, his shiny black shoes. But most of all, he noticed the shiny black nose of the puppy peeking out from the man's buttoned-up black overcoat. Charles watched the puppy's nose twitch.

Uncle Stephen cleared his throat and stepped forward. "I don't believe we've met," he said. "I'm Stephen DeVries, and this is my wife, Abigail, and my daughters, Beck —"

The stranger frowned and shook his head. "No time for all that. Look, can you help me or not?

I'm a busy man. I can't care for a houseplant, much less a dog. I figured you farm folks —" The puppy began to whimper and wriggle. The man adjusted his arms, trying to maintain his grasp, but it was clear to Charles that he didn't have a clue about how to calm a puppy.

Charles walked over and held out his arms. "I'm Uncle Stephen's nephew Charles," he said. That came out kind of funny, but he didn't care. All he could think about was that puppy, and how much he wanted to hold it. "I'm pretty good with puppies," he added. "Is it a girl or a boy?"

"A girl. I think. Who knows? I'm not even sure. It all happened so fast." Quickly, the man unbuttoned his coat and handed the puppy over with a look of relief. He pulled an oversized red silk handkerchief out of the breast pocket of his perfect black suit and used it to wipe his hands. Just then a phone buzzed. "That's me. Gotta take this." He stepped back, reaching into his pocket.

Charles smiled when he felt the warm weight in his arms. The puppy was really too big and too heavy for him to hold, so he let her down gently onto the floor and knelt next to her to pet her. "Well, hello," he said softly. The puppy was brown on top and white below, with half-pricked, half-floppy ears, four big white-stockinged paws, and a blaze of white right down her face. She gazed up at Charles, looking adorably worried with her wrinkled brow and big soulful brown eyes.

Who are you? Will you be my friend?

Lizzie, Becky, and Stephanie clustered around Charles to coo over the puppy, and the Bean reached around them to pet her. Buddy danced around, stretching his nose in to sniff the new arrival. The puppy wagged her tail; she seemed to enjoy all the attention.

Charles buried his nose in the puppy's neck. She smelled sweet, like cookie dough mixed with a horsey smell. She was a big, solid girl, with chunky paws. Her fur was unbelievably soft. She yawned, showing sharp white teeth and a tender pink tongue, and shook her head so her ears flopped. Then she sat up on her haunches and put her big paws on either side of Charles's neck, giving him a warm puppy hug as she sniffed and snuffled at his cheek. He felt his heart swell. "What a sweetie," he said. "Good girl."

"Good, good," the man echoed, but he was talking into his phone. "I'll be in touch." He snapped the phone shut and looked around like someone waking from a dream. When his eye fell on Charles and the puppy, he nodded curtly. "I'll be off, then," he said. He took a step away from the door.

"Wait!" said Uncle Stephen. "Are you leaving this puppy with us? Where did it come from? What are we supposed to do with it?"

The man began to button up his overcoat. "Look. I'm not a dog person, and I'm no hero. But here's what happened. I was working in the city today. Afterward, I'm on my way home, at rush hour, on a highway with four lanes of busy traffic. Next thing I know, there's this tiny thing trotting across the road, ignoring all the cars and trucks whizzing by. How she managed to avoid getting flattened like a pancake, I'll never know. Anyway, I pulled over onto the median, grabbed her, and —" He held up his hands. "That's all I know. End of story. Can you help me or not?"

Charles gaped at the man. "You *are* a hero," he said. "You saved this puppy's life."

The man shrugged. "Whatever." His phone buzzed again. He pulled it out of his pocket and looked at it, frowning. "Why can't they figure things out on their own?" he said to nobody. Then, without so much as a good-bye glance, he flipped the phone open and began to walk away. "Yes?" he said into the phone as he stepped off the porch. "What is it now?"

"Wait," said Uncle Stephen. "We don't even know your name."

But the man had disappeared into the dark November night.

"Who *was* that?" Mom asked.

"I don't know, and honestly I'm not sure I care to know," said Aunt Abigail. "He certainly was rude."

"I'm guessing he's one of our new neighbors," said Uncle Stephen. "Not too neighborly, I'd say."

"Very odd," Dad said.

The puppy whimpered, and everybody turned to look at her.

"Pretty funny that he came here, isn't it?" Lizzie petted the puppy and made soothing noises. "I mean, we foster puppies. That's what we do. But how could he know that?"

"Well," Mom said quickly. "Fostering puppies — that's what we do at *home*. We're just visiting here, remember?"

"But we *have* to help," said Becky. "Look at her. This puppy is adorable. And she's obviously all alone in the world. No collar, no tags, running around in traffic . . ."

"Poor thing," said Stephanie.

"We'd have to take her to the vet and find out if she has a microchip," Aunt Abigail said thoughtfully. "So many dogs have that now, and if she does, it's possible we could find her owners."

15

Charles stared at his aunt. He knew what a microchip was: a tiny computer chip that could be inserted under a pet's skin, with information about who owned the cat or dog and how to find them. But the way Aunt Abigail was talking . . . "You mean —"

Aunt Abigail and Uncle Stephen exchanged looks. Then they both smiled and nodded. "Yes," said Aunt Abigail. "In the spirit of Thanksgiving, I think we should help this puppy."

CHAPTER THREE

"Well, that's settled, then," said Aunt Abigail. "We'll have plenty of time to get to know the puppy, but for right now, let's get supper on the table. You all must be starving after your trip. And why don't you bring your things upstairs and get settled?" She waved a hand around at everything they'd carried in. "You're all in your usual rooms. Becky, Stephanie, come give me a hand in the kitchen." She bustled off, and soon everyone else scattered as well. Charles found himself alone with the puppy. She put up her paws to give him another hug, then sat down and looked at him, whimpering softly.

"What's the matter, sweetie?" Charles asked. The puppy shook herself off, then stretched and yawned, her front paws way out in front and her bottom in the air. Charles noticed the way her white-tipped tail curled over her back.

She was so cute. She shook herself again and began to pad around, sniffing here and there on the floor. "Uh-oh," said Charles. "Do you have to —" Just then, the puppy began to squat, right in the middle of the entryway floor. Charles swooped in and scooped her up. "Let's get you outside." He pushed open the front door and stepped out into the dark, cold night.

He had no leash, but he had no choice, either. This puppy needed to pee. He lugged her out onto the front lawn, put her down, and watched her closely. "Good girl," he said as she squatted in the ivy surrounding a big tree. "Okay, let's go back inside."

But the puppy had other ideas. She wandered further into the yard, away from the circle of light from the house, out into the darkness. "Puppy!" Charles called. "Come, puppy." His heart thumped in his chest. What if she ran off? This dog had run away before, into four lanes of traffic. Wasn't that enough for one day? "Come on, girl," he called into the dark.

Finally, he spotted her coming toward him, dragging something red and floppy along the ground. When she came closer, into the light, he realized it was a piece of red cloth — the silk handkerchief from the stranger's pocket.

He grabbed the puppy before she could get any more ideas about wandering around. "Give me that," he said, taking the handkerchief from her mouth. The heavy, smooth fabric felt cold. He shoved it into his sweatshirt pocket and headed back inside, herding the puppy in front of him.

"We need to get this puppy a collar and a leash," he announced as he walked into the kitchen with the puppy at his heels. "And a name."

Over dinner — Aunt Abigail's famous chicken and dumplings — the puppy was the main topic of conversation. "What breed do you think she is, Lizzie?" asked Uncle Stephen. He knew that Lizzie had practically memorized the "Dog Breeds of the World" poster that hung on her bedroom wall.

Lizzie shook her head. "I've been trying to figure that out." They all turned to take another look at the puppy, who was lying on a bed they'd made from some old towels Aunt Abigail had provided. She slept soundly, with her legs straight out in front of her. Once in a while her feet twitched and she let out a soft snore.

"Poor thing," said Aunt Abigail. "Whatever she is, she's all tuckered out. What a day she must have had."

"I think she looks like a Saint Bernard, only not so big," said Stephanie.

Lizzie nodded. "Or maybe a Bernese mountain dog. Same kind of coloring, brown and white. She might have some German shepherd in her, too. Look at her pointy snout, and the way her ears sort of try to stand up. She's definitely a mixed-breed. An all-American. A mutt."

"Mutts are the best." Charles glanced over at Buddy, who lay in another corner of the dining room on his own bed.

Buddy and the new puppy had similar coloring, brown and white, and their half-pricked ears were similar. Buddy's brown was a tan caramel color, while the new puppy's fur was darker, like strong coffee, but they both had a white stripe up the middle of their faces. Besides that, they were completely different. That was the great thing about mutts, thought Charles. Each one was unique, not exactly like any other dog in the world. Nobody knew what mix of breeds Buddy was, but he was the best puppy ever and they all loved him.

"Who cares what she is?" he said, looking at the new puppy. "She's really cute."

"So, what should we call her?" asked Becky. "How about Pilgrim, since she came at Thanksgiving?"

"Or Serendipity, for her good luck?" Dad asked.

"What would we call her for short, Dipity?" asked Mom, laughing. "I vote for something simple, like Daisy."

"Maybe we should try to figure out her real name," Charles said. "After all, she probably had one. We could call her lots of different names and see if there's one she responds to."

"That would take forever," said Lizzie. "What would we do, go alphabetically? Think about it. Abby, Addie, Aggie . . . that's just the *A*'s."

They argued about it straight through to dessert. "Who wants coffee with their pie?" Aunt Abigail asked as she cleared plates. "We just got a new espresso machine. I've been treating myself to a yummy mocha latte every night."

"What's that?" Charles asked.

"Coffee with foamy milk on top." Stephanie wrinkled her nose. "The foamy milk part is good, but the coffee — yuck."

"Mocha Latte," Charles said. "That's it! The perfect name for the puppy. She's brown and white, just like coffee and milk. We can call her Mocha for short."

Everybody stared at him. "What?" Charles asked. Maybe that had been a really dumb idea.

"You're right, it's absolutely perfect," said Mom, reaching out to give his hand a squeeze.

CHAPTER FOUR

First thing the next morning, Charles and Becky buckled up in the backseat of the van. In front, Mom drove as Uncle Stephen, in the passenger seat, gave directions. Charles could tell that, just like Lizzie, Mom did not like her little brother telling her what to do.

"Take a left out of the driveway," Uncle Stephen said as they started out.

"I know the way to town, Stevie," Mom answered. "I just don't know exactly where the vet's office is."

Becky and Charles smiled at each other. Then Charles turned around in his seat so he could see Mocha and Buddy, sharing the way-back. The two had already become such good pals that Charles had begged Mom to let Buddy come along.

Aunt Abigail had called the local vet and arranged a quick visit, just so he could check Mocha for a microchip. "If someone is missing this dog, they'll want to know where she is as soon as possible," she'd said. "If there's no microchip, then there's probably no way we can find her owners. At least we'll know one way or the other."

Now Charles reached back to pet Mocha. Poor little girl. Had she ever had a real family? "If we can't find your people," he promised her, "we'll find you the very best home we can." Mocha thumped her tail and licked his hand, gazing up at him with her big brown eyes beneath that cute wrinkled brow.

I'm not sure where I am, but I am sure of one thing: you're a friend.

Up front, Mom made a disgusted sound as they drove past the big stone pillars that flanked the iron gate. "We noticed that place yesterday. Who lives up there, anyway?" she asked. "Some millionaire?"

"I guess he must be," said Uncle Stephen. "That's our newest neighbor. The guy who owns it is probably the richest guy in the county. He likes his privacy, that's for sure. Nobody around here has ever seen him, much less met him. He drives through town in a big black car with tinted windows."

Becky leaned over to whisper to Charles. "Once," she said, "after I saw his car leave, I went right up to the gate. I was going to sneak around it and ride my bike up the driveway to see his house, but I couldn't. The whole property is fenced in, plus there are tons of signs everywhere about some alarm system."

Charles raised his eyebrows. "I guess he really doesn't want any surprise visitors."

Becky shrugged. "Maybe not. But I'm going back soon. There's an intercom on one of those pillars, and I'm going to push the button and see what happens. Maybe the gate will swing open automatically!" She grinned at him. "Are you in?"

Charles stared at her. "I — I don't know," he said.

She raised her eyebrows. "Dare you," she said. "Double dare."

"Um," Charles began.

"Turn right up here," said Uncle Stephen. "And then take that left. See the red barn? That's where we're going."

Charles leaned forward in his seat and stared out the window as if he were very, very interested in the view, hoping that Becky would not notice that he had not answered her dare.

But Becky wasn't finished. "I'm thinking he might be our mystery man from last night," she added. "Don't you want to find out?"

Charles shrugged. "Maybe. I guess. But what if there's a security camera? What if guards come out? What do we say if someone asks us what we're doing there?"

Now Becky shrugged. "We'll think of something," she said as Mom pulled up in front of the red barn. A sign on the door said ELVIS STRUNK: SMALL AND LARGE ANIMAL PRACTICE.

"A vet named Elvis?" Mom asked, giggling.

"He's supposed to be a great guy," Uncle Stephen said. "Let's go meet him."

Charles liked the vet right away. He was a tall, gangly man with a warm smile. "I'm Dr. Elvis," he said, shaking everyone's hand in turn. "And this must be our lost dog," he added as he helped Mocha up onto the high table in the center of a sparkling-clean exam room. She wagged her tail as he looked her all over, running his hands along her body. Then she sat back on her haunches and put her paws up on Dr. Elvis's shoulders to give him a puppy hug.

Another friend! Wonderful.

Dr. Elvis laughed and hugged her back. "You like to make friends, don't you?"

"She gets along with everybody," said Charles. He had met a lot of sweet dogs, but Mocha might be the friendliest ever. He told the vet how Mocha had been found near the city, running across a busy four-lane highway.

Dr. Elvis finished the exam, checking her ears, eyes, and mouth. "I'd say she's about six months old. She's skinny, but she looks healthy enough. No collar probably means no home, but since she's so friendly I bet she was able to find folks who gave her food. She may have been living on the streets in the city for quite a while."

He picked up a device that looked like an oversized TV remote and waved it over Mocha's body. Then he shook his head. "I'm not picking up a chip. Too bad. I can notify the police and put out the word to any vets I know, but if she was running by herself in such a big city, I doubt we'll be able to track down her owners — if she ever had any."

Mom sighed. "I think you're right," she said. "After all, if she had a family they might not even be from the city. She could have jumped out of any car or truck going down that highway."

"She sure is a fine-looking dog, though." Dr. Elvis stepped back to get another view. "Great temperament, too. She's very sweet. Judging by those big paws, she'll probably grow to be ninety to a hundred pounds, maybe more. Wonder what her mix is."

"We were trying to figure that out," said Uncle Stephen. "Saint Bernard, maybe?"

"There's an easy way to find out," said Dr. Elvis. "I just got a DNA testing kit. We can take a blood sample and send it to a lab. They'll tell us exactly what breeds she is."

"You can do that?" Charles asked. He had never heard of such a thing before.

Dr. Elvis nodded. "In fact, I'm offering it as a free special these days, just to see how it works. What do you say?"

"Can we test Buddy, too?" Charles asked. "Our puppy, I mean. He's in the car."

Dr. Elvis looked surprised. Then he smiled. "Sure. Why not?"

CHAPTER FIVE

"While we're at it, maybe we should get Buddy microchipped," Mom said. "We've been talking about that for a long time, and this is a good reminder that it's a smart thing to do. If Mocha had a chip, we could be calling her owners right now."

"But Buddy would never run away," said Charles.

Dr. Elvis shook his head. "I've known plenty of dog owners who said that and were proven wrong. You just never know. I think your mom's right. Better safe than sorry. The process really doesn't hurt the dog at all, if that's what you're worried about."

While Mom got Buddy from the van, the vet took some blood from Mocha's leg, using a big needle that Charles did not like looking at. Then he asked Charles to hold Mocha while he worked with Buddy. Charles sat down on a bench next to Becky, and Mocha jumped up next to him. He pulled her onto his lap. She did not seem bothered at all by the poking and prodding she'd been through. She wagged her tail and licked Charles's face. Then she put her paws up on his shoulders to give him a big warm puppy hug.

This is fun. I wonder what we'll do next?

Charles laughed as he hugged her back, then tried to help her settle down. She squirmed in his lap and snuffled at his pockets while Charles and Becky petted her, trying to keep her calm and quiet.

"Well, well, aren't you a cutie?" Dr. Elvis said as he lifted Buddy onto the table. With quick, confident motions, he took some blood, then used another needle — even bigger — to insert a tiny microchip under the skin on the back of Buddy's neck. "Done," he announced a second later. Buddy had not even whimpered. Dr. Elvis petted Buddy. "If I had to guess, I'd say this guy is part Jack Russell terrier and" — he stroked his chin — "maybe part chow? But we'll know more when the lab processes the blood sample. It'll take a few weeks, but I'll be in touch as soon as I have results on both dogs."

A few weeks! Charles wished they didn't have to wait so long. Not that it really mattered. Buddy and Mocha were fantastic dogs, no matter what breeds they were. He hugged Mocha close as Mom and Uncle Stephen gave Dr. Elvis their phone numbers and other information.

"Hey," said Becky in an odd voice. "Look what she just pulled out of your pocket."

Charles looked down at Mocha. There, trailing from her mouth, was the red handkerchief she had found outside the night before. The handkerchief that belonged to the mysterious stranger. He'd forgotten all about it after he'd stuffed it into his pocket.

"This is great!" said Becky.

"Great? Why?" Charles was not sure he liked the way Becky's eyes were gleaming. That usually meant he was in for an adventure — the kind of adventure that did not always turn out so well.

"Don't you get it?" She pulled the big silky square gently from Mocha's mouth. "Now we have the perfect excuse to ring the intercom button on the big gate." She took a closer look at the handkerchief. "Check it out. There's a monogram on it. 'A.M.I.' I wonder what those initials stand for." She began to run through some possible names. "Abe Morrow Inkpot. Arthur Madison Ishkabibble. Alexander Migglestone Iverson . . ."

Charles felt his stomach knot up. And it stayed knotted for hours.

Before they headed back to the farmhouse, Mom reminded Uncle Stephen that Aunt Abigail had asked them to go to the supermarket for a few last-minute items. "Oops," said Uncle Stephen, patting his pocket. "I forgot to bring the list she made. But I think I remember most of the things on it."

Becky and Charles waited in the van while Mom and Uncle Stephen did the shopping. Charles was quiet, but Becky chattered on about the handkerchief, the gate, the initials. She couldn't wait to go push that intercom button. "We'll go right after lunch," said Becky. "We can say we want to walk down to the store."

Charles loved going to the general store down the road. It was a warm and welcoming place, with a woodstove surrounded by tables and chairs where local folks liked to sit and chat while they drank coffee. The store wasn't a supermarket, but it had most of the basics, like eggs and milk and canned tomatoes, so Aunt Abigail often sent Charles and Becky to pick up some last-minute ingredient she needed. In the summer, they could buy ice-cream cones from the takeout window and sit on the porch overlooking the lake while they ate them. But today Charles knew the trip to the store was just an excuse.

"Stephanie will be suspicious," Charles said. "Remember when we were hiding Flash in the barn, and we kept going down to the store for dog food? Stephanie figured out that we were up to something." When they had found Flash, the border collie puppy, Charles and Becky had decided to keep him a secret. That had not lasted long, not with their busybody older sisters around.

"Let her wonder," said Becky with a shrug.

As it turned out, Stephanie and Lizzie were busy cutting out pictures to make holiday collages when Becky and Charles told their moms they were going to the store. "Great," said Aunt Abigail. "Can you get me one more stick of butter, and some lemons? They were on my list but *somebody* forgot." She made a face at Uncle Stephen, but she was smiling as she pushed back her hair with a flour-covered hand. Aunt Abigail had once been a pastry chef at a fancy hotel, and she loved to cook and bake.

"*Somebody* is very sorry, since *somebody* was looking forward to your lemon tart," said Uncle Stephen.

The kitchen was a mess, with flour spilled everywhere and pots and pans clattering as Aunt

Abigail bustled to and fro, mixing and stirring and preparing for the next day's feast. Charles could hardly wait for all the delicious desserts they would have. He went over to sniff an apple cake that sat cooling on the counter.

"Let's go," said Becky, pulling on his sleeve.

"Take the dogs with you, please," said Mom. "They could both use some exercise."

A few moments later, Charles held Mocha's leash and Becky held Buddy's as they headed down the long driveway. Charles eyed the corner of the red handkerchief trailing out of Becky's pocket. He was curious about its owner, too, but he still wasn't sure about this plan of Becky's.

Before he knew it, they were standing at the gate with the big stone pillars. The gate looked even more imposing now that they were right next to it. Its black iron scrollwork loomed over them, and the pillars on either side of it towered high above their heads. Charles's heart thumped in his chest as Becky held her hand over the large black button on the silver metal intercom. "Ready?" she asked.

Charles drew in a breath and nodded. "I guess," he answered.

Becky pushed the button.

Nothing happened.

She pushed it again.

This time, the intercom erupted with the unmistakable sound of a pack of vicious dogs, barking their heads off.

CHAPTER SIX

"Yow!" Charles jumped back, nearly tripping over Mocha. She stood, feet planted and her ears laid back, barking at the intercom.

Who's that? Who's that? You don't sound very friendly! If you try to hurt my friends, I'll fight you.

Buddy joined in the barking, too. "Let's get out of here," yelled Becky, turning to run back onto the road. Charles tried to follow her, but Mocha did not want to stop barking back at the inter-com dogs. Charles was stuck. He couldn't leave

Mocha, but he didn't want to stand there for even one more second. Any minute he expected a pack of slavering, sharp-toothed guard dogs — Dobermans, maybe, with their sleek bodies and bullet-shaped heads — charging down the long driveway toward him. All he wanted was to get away before he saw those white teeth and red tongues up close.

"Come on, Mocha." Charles pulled at her leash. "Please!" Finally — after throwing in a few growls for good measure — she turned and trotted along after him.

"Yikes," said Becky when they were safely on the road again. She glanced back at the gate and gave a little shiver. "Well, that answers one question, anyway. That's not where Mocha's rescuer lives."

Charles tried to catch his breath. He looked back, too. "What are you talking about?" he said.

His brain did not seem to be working so well. Becky wasn't making sense.

"He doesn't have dogs, remember?" Becky said, in a "duh, don't you get it?" kind of voice. "He said he can't even care for a houseplant. So anyway, that can't be his place. We'll have to keep investigating if we want to find out who he is."

Charles looked back at the gate. "I think I've had enough investigating for one day," he said. "Let's just go to the general store and get your mom's lemons."

Becky shrugged. "Fine," she said. She swaggered along, acting as though the dogs had not scared her one bit, but Charles noticed that she kept checking behind them as they walked.

The store was just as Charles remembered it: warm and inviting, with squeaky old wooden floors and rows of shelves packed with everything from boxes of spaghetti to furniture polish.

Charles could smell something delicious, maybe a pot of soup simmering on the stove. The only thing that was different was the woman at the cash register, making change for a customer. She had long gray hair and a nice smile, but she did not look familiar. "Where's Mrs. Daniels?" Charles whispered to Becky as they entered the store. Charles remembered Mrs. Daniels because she had always enjoyed hearing his latest knock-knock joke.

"She sold the store to Kim and Carolyn last July," Becky whispered back. "That's Kim. Come on, I'll introduce you."

"Are you sure it's okay to bring the dogs in?" Charles asked.

The woman at the counter heard that. She smiled. "We love dogs," she said. "And these look like two excellent pups." She reached into a glass cookie jar and pulled out two big dog biscuits.

"Here you go," she said, coming around the counter to give one to each dog, along with a pat and a kiss on the head.

"This is my cousin Charles," Becky said. "And the dogs are Buddy and Mocha."

"Hello, Buddy," said Kim. "Hello, Mocha. Aren't you a pretty girl?" She ruffled Mocha's ears. "Carolyn will love this dog," she predicted. "She had a husky once and she likes big pups with curly tails." She stood up. "Carolyn," she called. "Come meet some dogs."

Carolyn came out from the kitchen in the back of the store, wiping her hands on a long white apron. She had short curly gray hair and wore silver-rimmed glasses. She beamed when she spotted the dogs. "Well, hello," she said as she knelt to pet Buddy and Mocha. Mocha put two feet up on Carolyn's shoulders and leaned in for a puppy hug.

"Mocha!" said Charles. "Down, girl." Sometimes Mocha could be a little *too* friendly.

Carolyn laughed. "That's okay. I needed some puppy love today." She returned Mocha's hug and kissed her on the ear. Then she looked up at Kim. "Lots of orders coming in for food. Everybody's panicking with this ice storm they're predicting."

Kim nodded. "I know. We're almost sold out of toilet paper and milk already."

"Speaking of milk . . ." said Carolyn, straightening up. "Now that your dogs have had a treat, maybe you kids would like a snack, too. I just took a fresh batch of chocolate chip cookies out of the oven."

Charles and Becky looked at each other, shrugged, and smiled. Home-baked cookies? Who could say no to that? Soon they found themselves on a bench in the back of the store, backs warmed by the woodstove, munching on their sweet treats.

"Casey's Café." Charles read the sign over the counter. "Enter as strangers, leave as friends."

"Casey's Café is named after Kim and Carolyn. Their initials are K.C. Get it?" Becky asked.

People sat at tables, chatting as they spooned up soup or sipped hot chocolate. "The guy in the plaid jacket is Neil," Becky whispered, nudging Charles. "He drives the town's snowplow. And his wife, Dot, raises goats." She pointed to another man. "Wayne runs the gas station. Dad says he can fix anything. And that's Dean, next to him. He takes care of some of the vacation homes around here."

Buddy immediately curled up by the woodstove, but Mocha made her way around the table, saying hello to each person in turn, making friends out of strangers just like the sign said. Charles had never seen such a social dog. Each person in the café petted Mocha and cooed over her, and her tail wagged harder and harder.

A big burst of laughter came from the table. "No kidding," Charles heard the man named Dean say. "These second-home owners are helpless — and clueless, too." He leaned in toward the others. "You know those folks with the big stone house up on East Hill? I knew they were coming up for the holiday, so I got the place all ready, laid logs in the fireplace and everything. The guy calls me last night to ask where the switch is. 'Switch?' I asked. 'To turn on the fire,' he says. 'Try a match,' I told him."

Everybody cracked up. Becky and Charles grinned at each other. It was fun to eavesdrop on this conversation. "That's nothing," said Neil. "Remember that little old snowstorm we had last week, two inches of fluff? I plowed out that place up on Pleasant Street, but the guy was still too scared to drive down his own driveway. He called and begged me to tow him out to the main road."

"Can't wait to see how they all handle the big storm coming our way," said Neil.

Wayne shook his head. "If you want to live out here in the sticks, you gotta know how to do for yourself. And maybe help a neighbor, too. This town's going downhill fast if these are the kind of people moving in."

Becky finished her cookie in two big bites, gulped down the last of her milk, and raised her eyebrows at Charles. He wondered what she had in mind. He found out soon. She pulled the handkerchief out of her pocket and looked at the monogram in the corner. "Do any of those people you're talking about have the initials A.M.I.?" she asked when there was a lull in the conversation.

Wayne scratched his head. Neil looked up at the ceiling. Dean knit his brows. Then they all shook their heads. "Nope." "Can't think of anyone." "Ya got me."

Just then, Mocha pulled the handkerchief out of Becky's hand and ran to the door with it.

A roar of laughter went up from the table. "Nice move, pup!" said one of the guys.

"Guess that means it's time to get going," said Becky.

Charles and Becky leashed the dogs, zipped up their jackets, and headed home. "It doesn't sound like people like their new neighbors too much," said Charles as they walked. "Or, at least, they don't respect them."

"I know," said Becky. "I'm glad my mom and dad know how to do stuff. Wayne is right. Those people shouldn't live in the country if they can't take care of themselves." She turned off the road, onto a little path that wound through the woods.

"Where are we going?" Charles asked as Becky and the dogs charged ahead, leaping over roots and rocks. But Charles slowed down. Where was the road? Were they even headed in the right direction?

"This is the back way home." Becky turned to face him. She rolled her eyes. "Don't worry, I've taken this path a million times. We won't get lost."

Charles had to admit that Becky seemed to know her way. And sure enough, they soon found themselves back at the farmhouse. Aunt Abigail was wiping down the kitchen counter when they walked in. "Where are my lemons?" she asked.

CHAPTER SEVEN

When Charles awoke the next morning — Thanksgiving Day — he took a look out the window. Then he rolled over and snuggled down deep into the flannel-lined coziness of his sleeping bag, glad that he did not have anywhere to go. It was rainy and gray and cold outside. Charles didn't see any ice on the window, though. Maybe it was just a yucky day. Maybe the storm warnings were wrong.

Anyway, the good news was that Uncle Stephen had promised to go back to the store for the lemons Charles and Becky had forgotten. According to him, Carolyn and Kim always stayed open at least until noon on holidays just for last-minute needs like this.

When Charles finally got up and headed into the living room, Mom was watching the weather channel. "I don't know, Stevie," she told her brother. "They're still saying that temperatures are dropping and this rain will start to freeze. Why go out in weather like that unless you really have to?"

"I've got snow tires and four-wheel drive," said Uncle Stephen as he shrugged into his jacket. "I'll be fine."

He petted Mocha and Buddy. "You two are in charge," he told the puppies. "Make sure nobody gets into trouble while I'm gone." He turned to Aunt Abigail. "Need anything else besides lemons?" he asked. "Last chance."

Charles felt bad about forgetting the lemons, but he knew that Uncle Stephen enjoyed spending some time at the store most mornings, hanging out and chatting by the woodstove. The lemons were really just an excuse.

Aunt Abigail sat on the couch next to Mom. Both of them were peeling potatoes. She paused for a moment, thinking. "Nope," she said. "I think we're all set. And we really could live without the lemons, too."

"Are you kidding? Your lemon tart is my favorite. There's no way I'm missing out on that," said Uncle Stephen. He headed out the door and Charles watched from the window as his car puttered down the driveway. As far as he could tell, the car wasn't slipping or sliding, so there was no ice yet.

"Charles, how about giving us a hand?" his aunt asked. "It would be great if you could take these peeled potatoes into the kitchen and put them into the pot of cold water on the counter.

Then you can bring us the bag of carrots right next to it."

Charles looked around. Where were Becky, Stephanie, and Lizzie? Obviously, they'd all found better things to do — which left him stuck with being Aunt Abigail's servant for the morning. Actually, he didn't mind. He was used to helping out in the kitchen, and it was easy work.

Even though it was cold and gray outside, it was warm and snug inside. Mocha and Buddy snoozed near the living room woodstove and all the lamps were lit, casting a happy glow.

For the next hour or so, Charles was content to carry things back and forth, find things in the fridge, and search for things in the linen cabinet and the dish cupboard. His dad helped, too, and they joked and talked while they set up the extra card table and carried chairs in from other rooms.

"Well," said Aunt Abigail a little later, as she looked around the kitchen. "I'd have to say we're just about set." She took a long happy sniff. "That turkey is beginning to smell absolutely —"

Before she could finish her sentence, the kitchen went dark. "Uh-oh," said Dad. "That's not good."

Suddenly, it was very quiet in the house. The weather channel guy wasn't talking anymore. The fridge wasn't humming. The furnace wasn't whooshing.

Aunt Abigail opened the back door and stuck her hand outside. "Not good at all," she said. "It's still pouring — and now it's cold enough that it's all been turning to ice as soon as it lands. A tree must have fallen on a power line nearby."

Charles poked his head out. "Wow," he said. "It's kind of pretty." Every branch on every tree was already covered in a shining coat of ice. Ice coated the walkway to the barn. It coated the Petersons' van. It covered the bushes, the birdbath, and the little statue of a toad in the garden. Charles stepped out onto the back deck for a better look — and immediately went sprawling. The boards were covered in ice and as slippery as a skating rink. "Ow," he said, rubbing his behind as he reached up for his aunt's hand.

"Pretty, maybe. But very treacherous. I wish your uncle were home." Aunt Abigail frowned and pressed her lips together. "I wonder if the phones are working."

Back in the kitchen, she went straight to the phone on the wall. By then, Charles's mom and all three girls had gathered to find out what had happened. The Bean had just woken from a nap. He rubbed his eyes and whined, upset just because everyone else seemed to be upset.

Mocha and Buddy scampered around underfoot. They didn't seem worried at all. Aunt Abigail picked up the phone and listened. She shook her head. "No dial tone," she said. She let out a long sigh. "And even if Stephen remembered his cell phone, there's never any signal down there at the store."

Then she sprang into action. "Stephanie, Becky, round up all the candles in the house. Paul, can you bring some firewood in from the back porch? And, Charles, maybe you could check the wood-box in the living room and bring me an armload of small pieces that I can use for kindling. If we still want to have our Thanksgiving dinner, I'm going to have to fire up this old beast." She patted the big black iron cookstove that sat along one wall of the kitchen.

"That really works?" Charles asked. He had always thought it was just for decoration. It usually had some pretty old bowls displayed on its shelves, and a big vase of colorful dried flowers.

"Sure," said Aunt Abigail. "Not that I've used it much lately. But since it runs on wood, it's an excellent backup. I doubt my electric stove will be doing us any good today. When the power goes out like that — suddenly, all at once, without any flickering — it's usually a sign that it's going to be out for a while. Days, maybe."

Stephanie and Lizzie gasped, and Charles could imagine just what they were thinking. No phone? No Internet? No DVDs? He grinned. He could live without any of those things. This was going to be the kind of adventure he could enjoy.

"What about the food in the fridge?" Mom asked.

"It'll stay cold as long as we don't open the door too often," said Aunt Abigail. "If the power stays out for long, we might have to start setting things outside to stay cold."

Charles went to get the kindling, with both puppies trotting after him. When he came back, Aunt Abigail and Becky were just emerging from Aunt Abigail's pantry, each lugging two big gallon jugs of water. "I've got a dozen or so of these — we keep them filled just for emergencies like this," said his aunt. "Without electricity, our pump doesn't work. We'll have to make the water last. That means no bathing."

"And no flushing," Becky added.

"Well, just not flushing too often," said Aunt Abigail.

"It sounds as if you've been through this a few times," Mom said.

Aunt Abigail nodded. "It happens," she said. "It's not so bad."

"What about a generator?" Dad asked.

"We've talked about getting one," said Aunt Abigail. "Lots of folks around here have them.

They run on gasoline and you can start them up when you lose power. They'll keep everything going, from your fridge to your computer to your TV, but they're expensive and loud."

Before long, the living room woodstove had been stoked, and candles were lit all over the house. A fire crackled in the big black cookstove, and Charles and Becky sat at the kitchen table near its warm bulk, waiting for the hot chocolate Aunt Abigail had promised them. Mocha lay at Charles's feet in easy reach for petting, and Buddy snoozed by the cookstove. Everything was cozy and sweet, and all was well.

Except for one thing. Uncle Stephen was still not back.

CHAPTER EIGHT

Aunt Abigail paced up and down in the kitchen, a worried look on her face. Every so often she picked up the phone and listened, then put it back down. "I haven't heard the sanding truck go by," she said. "Maybe Stephen is just waiting until they've sanded the roads. That ice can be awfully slidy to drive on until they've spread sand or salt over it."

She nibbled at a fingernail. "It's weird, though. Usually the local road crew is on top of everything. They take great care of our roads, whether it's a holiday, the middle of the night, whatever. Normally Neil would have driven the town's big truck up and down our road at least a couple times."

"I'm sure everything is fine." Charles's mom spoke in the soothing tone she used when the Bean was upset about something. "You know Stephen. He's just hanging out down there, cracking jokes while he waits until it's safe to drive, that's all."

"Betsy's probably right," said Charles's dad. "But" — he glanced at Mom — "I'm starting to feel as if I ought to go check things out. If there's been some sort of emergency, I can help. I have my first-aid kit in the van."

Mom frowned. "How can you possibly drive on these roads?"

"I can't," admitted Dad. "I was planning to walk. I have those ice-gripper thingies I can attach to my shoes."

"Still, it's dangerous to be on the road," said Aunt Abigail. "What if a car comes along? They might not be able to stop in time even if they see you."

"You could go the back way," said Becky. "That would be even easier, because you can crunch through the layer of snow in the woods and fields."

Dad nodded. "Sounds good. But I've never gone that way."

"We'll show you." Becky jumped up. Mocha scrambled out from under the table, ready for action. "Charles and I took the path yesterday. I know the way really well."

Charles held in a groan. He was not exactly excited about going out into this yucky weather. Once again, Becky was pushing him past his comfort zone.

Dad thought about it for a moment. "Okay," he said finally. "I suppose it's not a bad idea to have a few people go, so that someone could come back with a message if we need more help. Or," he added quickly when Aunt Abigail's face fell, "to tell people back here that everything's all right."

Charles and Becky found their hats and gloves and put on their boots and jackets. Buddy was still curled up by the stove and barely lifted an eyelid, but Mocha pranced around, waving her curly tail and making eager dashes toward the door. "Why don't you take her with you?" Mom asked. "She needs to get outside at some point and burn off some of that puppy energy."

Aunt Abigail found two more pairs of "ice-gripper thingies," and Becky showed Charles how to stretch them over the bottoms of his boots. "Too bad we don't have any for Mocha," Becky said. "Good thing she has toenails."

Mocha's toenails didn't do her much good when she headed out the back door at full blast, only to go sliding off the porch and onto the crusted snow in the yard. But she picked herself up and shook herself off, her tail still wagging. She gave Charles a doggy grin.

That was kind of fun! Better than lying around all day, anyway.

Dad inched his way to the van and grabbed his first-aid backpack. He slung it over his shoulder and they set off. It took a while to get down the icy driveway. They walked along the sides, where the crunchy snow did give a little traction. But Charles could tell that one wrong step, even with the grippers, would mean a slippery, sliding fall.

The rain had stopped. A thick glaze of ice covered every branch of every tree so that their limbs drooped sadly. Some large branches had broken under the heavy weight and lay scattered about on the snow and in the driveway. Still, Charles thought it was beautiful, in a weird way. A bush covered with red berries, each one encased in ice, made a splash of color against the gray sky. The ice glittered even in the low light, and when the wind blew, you could hear the musical sound of thousands of ice-covered branches rattling against each other.

Crunch, crunch, crunch. Mocha led the way as they inched across the silent, empty road and found the beginning of the path through the woods. Fallen branches littered the ground, and Charles glanced up nervously as the trees above them creaked and swayed. "It sure looks different today," he said. He wondered if Becky would have a hard time finding the way.

Dad touched Charles on the shoulder. "Okay there, sport?"

"I'm fine." Charles reached down to pet Mocha, who walked by his side, picking her way through the snow. She glanced up at him happily, and he felt better. He had his new friend with him. And if Mocha wasn't worried, why should he be?

Becky moved confidently, following what was left of the path. Charles recognized a few land-marks: a big boulder, an old spreading tree near a stone wall, a stream that trickled between snowy banks. After about ten minutes in the woods, they came out into a field and crunched across the undisturbed snow. Then Becky veered toward a group of tall pines, now drooping under their icy coating. "Almost there," she told Dad.

A few moments later, Mocha pricked up her ears as they emerged from the pine grove. She pointed her nose toward a group of buildings that had come into view.

Charles recognized the store. They'd made it. But something looked different. As they got closer, Charles realized what it was. The towering maple tree that shaded the store's porch in summer had toppled across the road. One of its huge branches had smashed through the windshield of Uncle Stephen's car.

Dad hiked his first-aid backpack up onto his shoulders and began to run. "Stay back," he called over his shoulder to Becky and Charles. "Keep Mocha out of the way, and steer clear of any power lines that have fallen down." He sprinted toward the store, crunching through the snow.

CHAPTER NINE

Becky turned to Charles, her hand over her mouth. Her eyes were wide with fear.

"Don't worry." Charles touched her shoulder. "It'll be okay." He tightened his grip on Mocha's leash. "Come on," he said. "Let's go find out what's going on."

He led the way across the field toward the store. By the time they arrived at the side of the road, Dad had checked out the car. He stood up and waved to them. "It's all right," he said. "Nobody's inside the car. He must be in the store."

Charles felt Becky grab his hand. He let out a sigh of relief. "Your dad's fine," he told her. "The tree must have hit his car after he parked and went inside."

Becky began to run clumsily through the crunchy snow, and Charles followed her. They met Dad on the slippery porch of the store and all three of them pushed their way inside together. The lights were on there. Thick cables snaked through the store, delivering power from the generator that Charles could hear throbbing from underneath the floor, in the basement. Uncle Stephen sat in Casey's Café, near the woodstove with a group of men. He pushed his chair back and jumped up when they came in. Then he opened his arms to Becky, who ran toward him and buried her face in his chest. "Sweetie, what are you doing here?" he asked.

"We were worried." Her voice was muffled by his jacket. "You didn't come home."

Uncle Stephen patted her on the back and smiled down at her. "Well, now you know why," he said. "I guess my car's not going anywhere for a while. We tried to move the tree, but it won't budge. Then we had to push three cars in a row out of the ditch by the big turn. Now we're just trying to figure out what to do next. The town's truck is trapped behind that tree, so Neil can't sand the roads. Dean's truck is stuck up that long, steep driveway of his, and Wayne must be busy pulling folks out of ditches. I know your mom must be worried, but I didn't feel like I could leave until we worked this out."

Carolyn came over with a tray full of mugs. "Coffee? Hot chocolate?" she asked. "Oh, and look who came to visit again." She smiled down at Mocha. "I'll go fetch a dog biscuit." She put down the tray and headed toward the front of the store with the puppy prancing along behind her.

"Mocha already knows where the biscuits are," said Uncle Stephen. "She's right at home, isn't she?" He turned back to the others at the table. "So, what next? Can we think of anybody else with heavy equipment? We're going to need a truck or a tractor with a pretty good winch on it to move that tree."

Everybody thought for a moment. "Patrick?" said Neil. "He's just down the road. Doesn't he have an old tractor?"

Another man shook his head. "He took it apart this fall and never got it all put back together."

Kim came over with a plate of donuts. "Looks like we're all stuck here for a while," she said. "I can't provide a turkey dinner, but here's a snack, anyway."

Charles sat with his donut and hot chocolate, watching as Mocha visited with each of her new friends. He felt warm and sleepy, sitting next to the woodstove. He could see that this storm was causing trouble, and he knew that soon he and Becky should probably head back to tell the others that everyone was safe. But for the moment, he was happy to sit and see what happened next. Finally, Mocha curled up next to the woodstove and sighed a happy sigh. She was content, too.

Then Charles saw her head pop up. Her ears twitched and her eyes grew bright. "What do you hear?" he asked her. He listened, too. Over the noise of the generator, he heard a higher-pitched throbbing — the sound of an engine.

"Who's that?" Neil asked. "Sounds like a tractor."

Everybody ran to the door. There, trundling down the road, was a big green tractor, chains on its enormous tires. A man in black coveralls and a big fur hat was at the wheel. He drove toward the downed tree, then turned the tractor around and backed up until he was near it. He cut the motor. Then he swung himself down from his high seat and stood scratching his head as he surveyed the damage.

"Got a winch?" Uncle Stephen called from the porch as he pulled on his jacket.

The man nodded. He went to the back of the tractor, bent down, and started fiddling with something.

"Excellent," said Uncle Stephen. "We'll be able to attach a cable to that tree and pull it right out of the way," he explained to Charles. "I want you two to stay up here while we work, though."

Becky and Charles watched from the porch as the men clustered around the tractor, climbing up and over the fallen tree trunk and attaching a cable near a large branch. After a while, the man in the coveralls climbed back onto the tractor and started it up. The tractor's engine powered the winch, which began to turn slowly, taking up the steel cable. With a creak and a groan, the tree began to move.

"Watch out!" yelled Dad as the top of the tree slid off the hood of Uncle Stephen's car and landed hard on the snowy ground. Charles could feel the thump all the way up on the store's porch.

The winch kept turning, and the tree kept moving. As it got closer to the tractor, the man at the wheel pulled the tractor forward. Finally, the tree began to slide on the icy road. He drove the tractor right across the road and towed the tree into the field next to the store. A cheer went up when the road was clear. Neil and Uncle Stephen smacked a high five. Then Neil climbed into his big dump truck and started it up. "Got a lot of road to sand," he called out the open window as he saluted the man in the black coveralls. "Tremendous job. Thanks, pal."

Charles and Becky watched as everyone clustered around the tractor, talking excitedly. Then the driver climbed down and they shook hands all around before moving toward the store in a group. The man in the black coveralls pulled off his fur hat as he came up onto the porch.

Becky gasped. Her mouth fell open as she stared at the man. She looked at Charles and raised her eyebrows. Then she turned to the man and pulled something out of her pocket. "I think this is yours," she said, handing him the red silk handkerchief.

CHAPTER TEN

"It sure is," the man said, smiling. He reached out for the square of silk, but before he could take it, Mocha snatched it out of Becky's hand and ran off, her tail held high as if she was proud of her prize. Charles could tell by the way she looked over her shoulder that she wanted to be chased.

Ha, ha! Look what I have! Don't you want it?

They all watched and laughed as the puppy slipped and slid on the icy porch floor, tossing the handkerchief high into the air and catching it. She shook it, with little puppy growls. She let it fall to the floor and she rolled on it. She picked it up again and pranced around proudly.

"It's okay," said the man. "I have others." He stuck out his hand to shake Uncle Stephen's. "Sorry I was too rushed to introduce myself last time. Sometimes I get a little too caught up in business, even though I'm supposedly retired. Anyway, I'm Archie Ingalls."

Uncle Stephen introduced himself and everybody else. Then they all trooped into Casey's Café, where Carolyn had coffee and hot chocolate waiting.

"You did a great job with that tractor," Uncle Stephen said to Archie as he stirred cream into his coffee. "You obviously know your way around heavy equipment."

He nodded. "I've been around big trucks and machines all my life," he said. "I'm a builder."

"Ingalls Construction!" said Dad. "You're *that* Ingalls. The one who built all those skyscrapers in the city, and that new museum, and the hospital —"

Archie Ingalls looked down at his cup. "That's right," he said. "I started out at sixteen, hammering nails. Worked my way up and eventually bought the company." He shook his head. "I retired a few years ago — or at least, I tried to. Turns out I can't stand to have time on my hands. That's why I came out on the tractor today — I couldn't get into the city, my cell phone was dead — I just needed something to do." He grinned. "Had to bust through my fence. That silly iron gate was stuck shut without the power on. I don't know why I ever put that thing up. I'll be taking it down as soon as all the ice melts."

Charles and Becky exchanged glances when they heard the word "gate." Charles raised his eyebrows, and Becky nodded.

"We can use a guy like you around here," Carolyn was saying. "There's always lots that needs doing in a town this size. I've been thinking about a community garden for next spring. Do you have a tiller attachment for that tractor?"

He nodded. "A snowplow, too. I was thinking I could plow out a pretty nice skating rink on that lake."

"That would be fantastic!" said Kim. "The kids around here would love that, wouldn't they, Becky?"

Charles looked over at Mocha, lying near the woodstove with her head on the red handkerchief. Maybe she belonged with the guy who had saved her life. "Taking care of a dog would keep you busy, too," he suggested. "Mocha still needs a home."

But Archie Ingalls held up his hands and shook his head. "Not ready for that kind of responsibility," he said, laughing.

"But wait. If you live behind that gate," said Becky, "what about those barking dogs we heard?"

Archie Ingalls gave her a look. "So that was you, pushing my doorbell the other day?"

"We just wanted to return your handkerchief," Becky said in a small voice.

He laughed. "The dogs are a recording," he said. "Another ridiculous idea. It's not like I need high security for my little cabin, is it?" He told them about the cabin he had built at the top of that long driveway. "Made it from trees I cut down myself, all from my own land," he said proudly. "The place is tiny, but it's all I really need."

Carolyn had a thoughtful look on her face. She turned to Charles. "Is Mocha available for adoption? I thought she belonged to you."

Charles and Becky took turns telling Mocha's story. Archie Ingalls looked into his coffee cup, embarrassed, when they said what a hero he had been to snatch her out of the way of speeding traffic.

By the time they finished, Kim and Carolyn were looking at each other and nodding. "We've been wanting a dog for a while," Kim said. "A general store needs a dog, a meeter and greeter for all our customers. And Mocha is so friendly, and so mellow. She'd be a perfect store dog. Do you think she'd like it here?"

"Are you kidding?" Charles asked. He knew Mocha would be in heaven, making new friends every day. "Look at her."

Mocha lay by the woodstove, gnawing on a chunk of firewood. She looked back at the group of smiling faces and thumped her tail.

* * *

Weeks later, the Petersons were still talking about it. "That was the best Thanksgiving ever," said Charles to his mom one afternoon just before Christmas.

"Archie Ingalls didn't even seem to mind that there was no lemon tart," Mom teased. "Those pies that Kim and Carolyn brought made up for it, didn't they?"

Charles nodded. It had been fun to see everyone gathered around the big table, lit by candles all down the center. The house had been cozy, warmed by two woodstoves, and even without any power Aunt Abigail had managed to create a memorable feast. She had not been fazed for one second when Uncle Stephen brought home three extra guests. She just told Stephanie to find a few more chairs and they were all set.

"I think Mocha found a great forever home, don't you?" Charles asked his mom.

"I do," said Mom. "And now when we go up there, Buddy can visit *his* cousin, too." She smiled at Charles.

Dr. Elvis had called them with the DNA results just that day. It turned out that Mocha was part German shepherd, part Bernese mountain dog, and part beagle. Buddy was mostly golden retriever and Jack Russell terrier — and also part beagle!

Charles reached down to pet Buddy's soft ears. "No matter what you turned out to be, I would love you just the same," he told his puppy. "You're one hundred percent fantastic." Charles's Thanksgiving had been full of adventures, but he was happy to be home.

PUPPY TIPS

If you find a lost dog, it's important to do everything you can to find her owners. You can put up signs, notify the police, and make sure that your local vet and humane society know about the found dog. Since Mocha was lost on a big highway in a big city, it would have been next to impossible to find her owners — if she even had any. But in a smaller town or neighborhood, your chances would be a lot better. Keep trying, the way Charles and his friend David did when they found Lucky, the lost mutt. Someone might be very, very happy to have their dog back home with them.

Dear Reader,

Mocha is based on a real puppy I know, whose name is also Mocha. She belongs to Kim and Carolyn, who run the general store near me. She greets everyone who comes into the store with enthusiastic kisses, tail wagging, and — for her special friends, like me — puppy hugs. Mocha is a sweet, happy girl. I love to take her for walks, and last summer I taught her how to swim in the lake.

The part about how the Mocha in this book was found, while she was running across traffic, came from a true story about the way my friend Cisco found his dog Woofy. I made up the parts about the rich neighbor, Dr. Elvis, and the ice storm. That's how a story gets made sometimes: a few real parts plus a few made-up parts equals fiction!

Yours from the Puppy Place,
Ellen Miles

P.S. Check out BANDIT, an adorable puppy found at a highway rest stop restaurant.

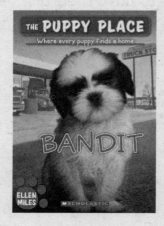

DON'T MISS THE NEXT PUPPY PLACE ADVENTURE!

Here's a peek at OSCAR!

The Bean put both hands over his mouth and watched, his eyes dancing, as Buddy licked every drop of syrup off Lizzie's plate, then went after Charles's. "Mine, too!" he said, holding up his plate so that syrup began to drip onto his lap.

Quickly, Lizzie grabbed it and put it down for Buddy. "There you go," she said lovingly. Buddy's tail wagged so hard that it thumped against

Lizzie's chair. He vacuumed up every bit of syrup, then sat back and licked his lips as he looked hopefully at Lizzie. "That's it," she said, holding up her hands. Mom and Dad never seemed to end up with extra syrup on their plates.

She hummed as she cleared the table and stuck the dishes into the dishwasher. Like her mom, she was looking forward to a nice, relaxing Sunday. Lizzie had been really busy lately, between school, volunteering at the animal shelter, and her dog-walking business. She and her best friend, Maria, were partners in AAA Dynamic Dog Walkers, and they walked about a dozen dogs every single day after school. Even dog-crazy Lizzie had to admit that sometimes it all seemed like a little too much.

"Hey, Lizzie, want to —" This time, Charles stopped himself. "I mean, hey, Beautiful Genius, want to play catch out back?"

"No, thanks." Lizzie was really enjoying her Pickle Jinx name. "I'm going to work on my scrapbook." Lizzie kept a scrapbook of all the puppies the Petersons had fostered, and it needed updating.

She was up in her room, pasting in a picture of a sweet, energetic chocolate Lab named Cocoa, when the phone rang. "Lizzie!" called her mom after a few minutes. "It's your aunt Amanda. She needs your help with a puppy."

ABOUT THE AUTHOR

Ellen Miles loves dogs, which is why she has a great time writing the Puppy Place books. And guess what? She loves cats, too! (In fact, her very first pet was a beautiful tortoiseshell cat named Jenny.) That's why she came up with a brand-new series called Kitty Corner. Ellen lives in Vermont and loves to be outdoors every day, walking, biking, skiing, or swimming, depending on the season. She also loves to read, cook, explore her beautiful state, play with dogs, and hang out with friends and family.

Visit Ellen at www.ellenmiles.net.